EXERCISES
FOR NON-ATHLETES
OVER FIFTY-ONE

EXERCISES
FOR NON-ATHLETES
OVER FIFTY-ONE
IT'S NEVER TOO LATE

WRITTEN AND ILLUSTRATED BY

OLGA LEY

SCHOCKEN BOOKS · NEW YORK

First Schocken paperback edition 1987
10 9 8 7 6 5 4 3   87 88
Copyright © 1985 by Olga Ley

Library of Congress Cataloging in Publication Data
Ley, Olga, 1912–
Exercises for non-athletes over 51.
    1. Exercise for the aged.   2. Physical fitness for the
aged.   3. Movement education.   I. Title.
GV482.6L49   1985   613.7'0240564   84–22238

Designed by Cynthia Basil
Manufactured in the United States of America
ISBN 0-8052-3979-0 (hardcover)
ISBN 0-8052-0834-8 (paperback)

Consult your doctor before doing any of the exercises.
It might be a good idea to show the doctor the book
since "exercise" can mean many different things.

CONTENTS

INTRODUCTION

Before you begin doing any of the exercises in this book, please read this chapter carefully so that you know exactly how you should do them.

First and foremost, they are to be done *slowly* and smoothly but thoroughly, so that you feel which muscles are working. Though you put as much effort into the movements as you are capable of, never force any movement to the point of pain.

Exercising should feel pleasurable, and it should teach you to enjoy moving. At this point I always say, watch cats. See what pleasure they get from a long complete stretch, and how relaxed and comfortable they are afterwards. No one has told them to stretch and exercise, and yet I have yet to see a cat that did not do so into extreme old age.

If you don't learn to enjoy movement you will soon drop any exercise program you undertake. If you have the self-discipline to do some twenty minutes of exercise a day music is a big help. For this type of movement violent rock and roll will not do. For my classes I use slow classical or romantic music, not so much to follow but to set the mood.

Never rush, avoid all abrupt and jerky movements, and under no circumstances bounce. I have spent some forty years saying monotonously, "don't bounce!" Bouncing (which is taught by many) is *not* a stretch. It gives one an illusion of stretching when it actually yanks the muscle with no control, increasing the possibility of injury; and the rebound, like snapping a rubber band, shortens the muscle without in any way increasing its flexibility.

One of the hardest things to get yourself to do is to make time for exercises every day, but it really is the best thing for you, especially if you are no longer young. If you just can't get yourself to do it, I have included many movements you can incorporate here and there, thereby using your body and moving until you begin to be acquainted with your body—as most people over a certain age are not.

The main problems of the aging body are bad posture and lack of flexibility. The bad posture is usually due to weak back and abdominal muscles, and back stiffness. Also, an amazing number of people keep their head forward and down, thus throwing their entire body out of line. The extent to which this is true, is shown by the fact that many ready-made suits are built with extra fabric across the back of the neck and shoulders to allow for round shoulders.

For this reason you will find many of the exercises in this book stress good posture and the strength and flexibility needed to maintain it. Good posture does not merely improve your looks, it is needed for the functioning of your entire body. It expands your chest, allowing your lungs to fill with more oxygen, and your inner organs to work better. It makes it easier for you to perform your daily tasks. Even if your body is far from ideal, you can improve it as long as you are still capable of moving. However, you must learn to *enjoy* movement, because unlike a piece of furniture, you can't fix up your body and leave it alone from there on in.

You will notice that I show most of the exercises

done with the feet flexed and *not* pointed. There is a reason for this. When you point your feet you contract the calf muscles and thereby lose the very important stretch along the back of the leg. A good many people have shortened hamstrings and Achilles tendons. Pointed toes do look lots prettier, especially in pictures, and I do use them for some exercises. When my exercises are done lying on the back with arms out on the floor you *must* keep the back of the hands on the floor and the palms up and try to keep the entire arms and shoulders in contact with the floor. Keeping the palms on the floor allows you to roll the shoulders forward, and this interferes with the expansion of the chest. You should also keep the elbows straight when the arms are extended overhead or outwards, unless told otherwise. Some of these things are difficult at first, but luckily muscles are not made of concrete and do eventually give.

The illustrations will in some cases show only one side of the movement, but since obviously you have an arm and a leg on each side you do both or, as my daughter once said when she was little, otherwise you will wind up "lump" sided. Since most people have a dominant side, the other one is apt to be both stiffer and weaker. If you find this to be the case do the "bad" side a few extra times.

You do not need to do the movements a great number of times. If done well and with conviction, half a dozen repetitions are ample, increasing possibly to double that. It is much better and less boring to try a variety, and then develop a repertoire of the ones that feel best for you.

You should also bear in mind that all the movements you make should originate in your body and flow to the extremities, and not the other way round. In other words, if you stretch an arm up and back, the movement does *not* begin in your hand. The first thing that moves is your shoulder, next the arm comes up, and the last part to rise is the hand. This flow of movement from the center of your body outward is what gives you control of your entire body. It is what makes dance look so beautiful. Dancers acquire this ability unconsciously as part of their training, but you should think about it as you move and practice until it becomes part of you.

There is no special virtue in sore muscles, though I have heard dancers boast about how sore they were. People have said to me that they were not sore after my class, and they wondered if they had done the movements in the wrong way. The point is that I don't expect anyone to hurt after doing my exercises. If you do them slowly, and do not repeat any of them too many times you should not feel any pain. Using your muscles in different ways usually prevents soreness. You might feel some muscle twinges, but that is natural if you haven't done anything of the sort for a long time. You should, anyway, get into a warm bath on the day you begin exercising, and stay in it for awhile. If you do feel some pain you won't feel it until two days later. Warm baths, and the "hair of the dog" in the form of some good stretches should prevent pain. There is one thing I want to warn you about. If you haven't used your abdominal muscles for a long time you might get cramps in the form of small painful knots in your belly when you bend down. If this occurs, all you have to do is to lean back, raise your chest, and stretch. The cure will be instantaneous.

If you are subject to cramps in your calves at night,

make a stirrup of your sheet, place the front part of your foot in it, and straightening the knee, pull the toes toward you. If you make sure that you do some of the leg stretches during the day, chances are you will be less apt to get the cramps at night.

I have drawn women in my illustrations, simply because having more women students, I find them more familiar to draw, but I assure you "La difference" makes very little difference. These exercises are strictly unisex. Older men have the same problems as women, the only difference I find is that by and large they are stronger and stiffer than women. It is rare that I have to modify an exercise for a man. I do teach fewer men than women, but there are still a great many of them. The difference is that at first they have to get used to my tempo, since most men's idea of exercise is to work themselves into a lather as fast as possible. Many of them are middle aged, or more, and they have been brought to me after they threw themselves too passionately into jogging or tennis.

IT'S NEVER TOO LATE

I have been teaching movement or exercise for some forty years, and in the course of the years my following, like me, has gotten much older. When I first began there were very few older people who would even think of attempting to do anything like exercise. In those days, once you reached middle age you subsided into physical immobility because you were convinced that you were beyond anything of the sort. Very few doctors then would have dreamed of suggesting exercise to an older person. Nevertheless, seeing my dance teachers moving freely and staying supple well into old age and knowing how wonderful movement made me feel, I was not surprised when I achieved the same results with the brave older people who were willing to take a chance. One student told another and I found that I had become a specialist in rescuing older people from creeping inertia.

The medical profession has now discovered the benefits of keeping older people moving instead of passively accepting physical incapacity, and today, doctors are urging them to exercise. Magazines and newspapers now extoll exercise as the best way for older people to keep fit. However, most of these publications are illustrated by 110-pound nymphets doing what is both threatening and impossible to an older person totally unused to the idea of even walking briskly. The result is, older people are frightened off. On television they see young things in leotards kicking and leaping to disco music, which is alien to them, and this frustrates them even further. Still, they are urged to exercise.

Exercise, it is now discovered, prevents osteoporosis in postmenopausal women, and in older men, helps combat the pain and stiffness of arthritis, keeps weight off, improves the circulation, straightens the spine, and even helps to cure those unexplained but chronic backaches, strengthens abdominal muscles, and generally makes people feel and look better, and may help prolong life. It is even found to relieve depression.

The trouble is that an aging body cannot be treated like that of a twenty year old. Muscles which functioned effortlessly at twenty become stiff or flabby in the later years and need special handling to get going again. Joints have become stiff, too, and at times painful, weight has accumulated here and there. All this requires a special approach, which is effective but not taxing. Through my training and experience I have developed my own system to handle these problems. I have enough knowledge of the body to cope with problems as they come up. Many of my pupils have been given exercise charts to follow at home, which I write and illustrate for them, and this enables them to work by themselves. These charts differ. Some are for actual exercises that they do fifteen minutes a day or so, and there are others which I call sneaky—those you can sneak into any daily activity. The latter are especially useful as they teach a person to know her or his body, and learn to *enjoy* movement. They are also fine for those who haven't the willpower or discipline to do actual formal exercises by themselves. They can be done at any time, and there is no way to overdo them. These charts work so well that I have often thought that assembled they would make an excellent book for those who have no access to classes. They are clear, easy to follow, and the illustrations though correct and forceful are not grim anatomical graphs, but are appealing, and sometimes even amusing.

These home exercises do not need any special equipment. If you have a straight chair, a bed, a floor, walls, a kitchen sink, a bathtub, a door, or anything of that type, I supply exercises to do with them. If you happen to be a dedicated exerciser I suggest you get one or two chinning bars which are available in sporting goods stores. They are used in doorways and it takes seconds to put them up or take them down. As to clothing, anything soft and knitted like a T-shirt and shorts or sweatpants is fine. If you want to be chic and classical you get a pair of tights and a leotard (if you can stand the sight of yourself in one). If you are alone you can work in your underwear. If you want to wear shoes they should be soft, heelless, and flexible. Dance slippers are best, but you can exercise in bare feet. It is very useful to have a full-length mirror to see what you are doing, but this is not absolutely necessary. Put a folded blanket under your back when you lie on the floor. You do not need expensive paraphernalia.

Now that older people are so much more numerous, and their needs are finally being recognized, there have been some books of exercises published for them. However, the approach of these works is usually unduly clinical, and tends to be pedantic and dull. This book is light, and optimistic. I want to stress that if a person is old, he or she need not be a vegetable. You will not be, or look sixteen again, it would be silly to suggest it, but you can look and feel better and be an example of what can be achieved at your age. Naturally, the book contains results of all my years of experience of working with older people, and you will find that all the exercises described here are well within your capabilities.

Most exercise books stress youth and beauty. I stress joie de vivre and not just technical exercise. Exercises are just the means to an end, the end being a better and more flexible and youthful body which people will enjoy all their lives. The point is not just to go through a routine of exercises, and then forget all about it the rest of the time. That is why I prefer the word *movement* to *exercise*, since movement is life and should be with you at all times. These movements are not heart stressing, though they do make your heart beat a little faster. Movement is possible as long as you have a muscle to move. I have taught movement in a home for the aged, and even they derived pleasure and benefit.

This book is for older people who for one reason or another do not exercise, or even move much, but who *know* that they should do so. The world has changed, the old are no longer silent and invisible, they live longer and more interesting lives than was once the case.

It is true that there is a small minority of older people who are physically active, and have always been so, and who do the same sports and activities as the young. But they are few and far between. They do not need me or my book.

But there are great numbers of older people who have given up, and who do not know how to move.

They can't imagine themselves tearing through the streets in running gear. On television gyrating young things in leotards scare them to death. This book is for them because it is nonthreatening and nonstressing. It is a pleasant way to make the most of your body at any age. The exercises do not stress the heart, they are to some extent aerobic, since they make you breathe deeper, and you can do them quietly and privately at your leisure. The results do not occur overnight, but I promise you they do occur.

EXERCISE TO LOSE WEIGHT

If you are expecting to lose weight by exercise the process will be so slow that you will see little change as you step on the scale every day. You will look trimmer, feel and look better, lose some flab and bulges, but you'll get frustrated by the slowness of your weight loss. The reason for this is that muscle tissue is dense and fat is not. As you build better muscles they outweigh the fat you lose; as a result the scale shows little change, but measurements will change visibly.

You should *not* go on a diet, and I shan't recommend any. A new one appears every month in the media. All diets work for a time. You lose weight rapidly, preen yourself on your success, and just as rapidly put it back on, as you resume the eating habits that put the weight on in the first place. What happens then is that you are on an endless seesaw, losing and gaining hundreds of pounds and getting nowhere.

The thing to do is to exercise or simply move more and eat as you always do, but *less*. Cut out some of the things that you know put weight on, or at least make the portions smaller. Stay away from pastry, if that is your downfall, for a week and then reward yourself with a piece on Sunday. Mathematically, if you put less fuel into your body and keep expending it by exercising you will lose weight. It might take you a whole year, but by then you will be so used to eating less and moving more, that the weight loss will stay with you for the rest of your life.

What's known as "spot reducing" can be done, since active muscles do not accumulate fat much, but it is a slow process, and your whole body will be toned and firmed before you see specific spots reduced.

At the same time, if you diet and don't exercise you will remain flabby and certainly nothing will happen to your posture, nor will you use your body any better. So you must gird your loins and make up your mind that if you want to stay in reasonable shape, there is no other way than through both exercising and restraining your appetite.

I don't think I need to tell you about good nutrition, this information is not only available but is thrust on you every day. Good "natural" eating is definitely *in*.

The number of health food stores testifies to this, and people pop vitamins by the millions. Someone has said that Americans have the richest urine in the world.

RUNNING OR JOGGING

Running for health has become a major sport. Thousands (and probably millions) of people are running every day. The word *aerobic* has become a magic means to well-being. Anything that makes you sweat, flail your arms, and kick your legs is aerobic. Jogging is, of course, as aerobic as can be. It also stresses the heart and makes your pulse race. All this is very good for you—*if* you are in good health to begin with, and have been physically active all your life. If, however, you have been sedentary and are fairly advanced in age you should think twice before tearing out into the street without first getting a thorough examination by a doctor. It is true that there are quite a few older people who run every day and benefit by it, but there are not too many of them.

Jogging, unquestionably beneficial, has several drawbacks. First of all, the majority of elderly people can't possibly visualize themselves running through the streets in running gear. You can jog with whatever posture problems you have, but the result is often backaches and pains in the neck. Jogging does not make you limber, on the contrary it tightens your muscles, unless you do a good stretching warm-up first, and another one when you are finished. In my studio I have seen passionate runners with tendonitis in their Achilles tendons, bad backs, sore feet, and calf muscles that felt like raw potatoes stuffed in them.

One habitual marathon runner, brought to me by his fiancée, after I had persuaded him to cut down on his mileage while I unknotted him, said to me as casually as if he were discussing a broken fingernail, that he no longer had any blood in his urine. When he noticed my reaction to this statement he said that it was nothing to worry about, just some mechanical irritation from the kidneys being jounced around. Many of his running friends had that condition too. It goes away if you rest for a while!

I also know of a man approaching fifty, who runs religiously every morning unless something dire prevents him. He does it with a group of friends. He has out distanced them, having started modestly some two years ago. He returns home glowing with health and euphoria. But he also returns with such excruciating pain in his knees that he has to first treat them with ice bags, then with heat, and after that he sits in a hot tub for some time. To his wife's suggestion that he see a doctor, he replies that it's not necessary. The pain is just payment for his health and pleasure. Besides, the pain goes away by the afternoon.

In my studio I see quite a few people who run habitually and love it. They come to me for stretching and posture work as a supplement to running. They appear hale and happy as well as undamaged. Not a single one of them is over forty-five.

The trouble with running as with many other fads in our country is that if a thing is "in" you must get with it, and Lord knows running is "in." There have been other epidemics like this before, after some time they are "out" and something else takes their place. Usually a smallish number of people stay faithful and go on, but the majority drop out. Also, every one of these fads becomes an industry with all kinds of equipment to go with it, and publications devoted to it, to say nothing of all the television shows that feature it.

I always suggest that my older students *walk* instead of trying to run, especially if they haven't done anything athletic for a long time. You can get the same aerobic benefit from walking as you can by running. All you have to do is be systematic, and do it right. First of all concentrate on your posture while walking, make it as good as you can, take deliberate, deep breaths, walk with vigorous strides, make them as big as you can, and wear low-heeled flexible shoes. Make a habit of it, devote some part of every day to it. Try to make each walking period a little longer. If you tire easily, stroll slowly for a block or so, and then resume the more vigorous stride. Don't set impossible goals for yourself, just do as much as you can. You will find that you will improve and enjoy it as you get stronger. A good way to get used to walking is to walk partway to wherever you need to go, or find some pleasant or interesting place to walk.

If worst comes to worst, put on your radio or record player, open a window, and walk in as big a circle as your living quarters allow. You can even "walk" in one place, doing what's known as marking time. Just remember to keep your chest up, breathe deeply, and don't let your head droop.

Here are two devoted runners each enjoying the activity. He is intense and serious, she is proud and smug. Neither of them is remotely aware that there is anything wrong.

It is how you do something that counts. Here are two ways of walking: The drawings are self-explanatory.

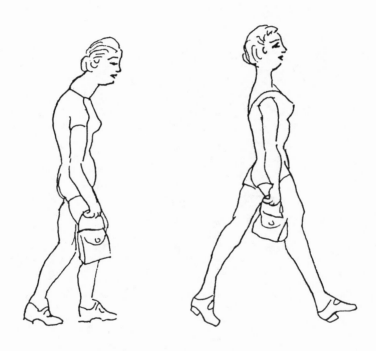

THE EXERCISES

SNEAKY EXERCISES

All of my exercises have been done in my classes by people as old as eighty with reasonable success, so I know you can do the same. Quite a few of my older students do them better than some of the young ones. If, however, you know that you can't get yourself to do a set of exercises faithfully every day (I know how hard that is for some people), then do the following "sneaky" ones and work them in whenever you can. First thing you know you will begin to feel your body moving and enjoy it.

This is one of the ways of remembering good posture: Stand with the best posture you can achieve. Holding this position tie a thin string, not around your finger, but around your waist. Make it fit snugly, but not really tight. As soon as you slump, the string will give you a gentle reminder to straighten up.

You can do some quite invisible exercises while standing in line at the supermarket, or waiting to get into the movies. Turn your toes in (somewhat pigeon-toed). Your feet should be a couple of inches apart. Pretend that you are going to turn your knees out, away from each other, keeping your knees straight. Now reverse the movement by turning your toes out, and trying to bring your feet together. Your feet will remain immovable, but you will feel everything tighten below the waist.

Sitting in any vehicle, public or private, press the small of your back against the back of the seat and turn the head as if looking out of the window. You can also press the balls of your feet down, and lift your heels; then reverse by bringing your heels down and lifting your toes. You can do the hand exercises while watching television, and if you are in a theater you can do them and no one will see you. You can stretch in bed and make a habit of it. It is a perfectly natural thing to do, even if you don't sleep alone. If you reach up to a high shelf exaggerate the stretch and reach higher than you need to.

You might also do well to notice how you sleep. If you sleep on your back, put a bolster of thick pillows under your knees to relax your back. Use only one thin pillow, or better still, none. If you sleep on your side, in what is known as the fetal position, which is, by the way, best for lower back pain, use two pillows so that your head remains on a line with your spine and your shoulders don't curl up around your ears.

If you sleep prone on your stomach, which puts a strain on your lower back, place a bolster or thick pillow under your belly, this will keep the small of your back from caving in. Since it is practically impossible to change the way you sleep after a lifetime of sleeping a certain way, you might as well make the position work for you instead of against you.

If you are used to reading in bed, you should get a slanted backrest which is available in different heights, and takes different forms. They are sometimes like an adjustable easel, or else at a permanent height and stuffed like furniture, in which case you will have to find the height which is best for you. There are as well plastic inflatable backrests, but they usually come in only one height. You will feel how comfortable it is to read with one of these, and how much better it is than propping yourself up on a sliding heap of cushions, which is really awkward and tiring.

When you bend down to put your shoes on, or pick something up, bend your knees and then leave your hands down and straighten your knees; straighten up, uncurling your back in the process. While combing your hair bring your elbows up and out. Look through the exercises and see which ones you can do en passant, such as the chest stretch you do in the doorway.

You can strengthen the muscle on the back of your arm between the elbow and the armpit by pressing the outside of your hand down on a table or any other firm surface. When you carry something fairly heavy, try to hold it with the pinkie and the next two fingers and not the thumb and index. If at the same time you let that arm hang, lift your chest, and turn the hand with the palm facing forward, you will help your posture. Make sure that when you carry things, or wear a shoulder bag, you change sides often, or else you will wind up with one shoulder higher than the other.

It is very difficult to lose an ingrained bad habit such as walking with your head down. You have to be compulsive about correcting the habit for a while, and if you persevere a good new habit will replace the old one.

You will find many exercises in the book that you can incorporate in your daily activities without taking time to do a group of them separately. The idea is to keep moving as much as possible in everything you do. The most destructive thing you can do to yourself is to become inactive, and passively let your body deteriorate. If you wear a girdle don't depend on it to hold you together. It probably feels reassuring, but if you think it's improving your figure, it isn't. Actually, it is making you flabby. If you do wear one, whenever you think of it, sitting or standing, contract your buttock and abdominal muscles as if shrinking inside the girdle. This will teach you to rely on yourself to improve your figure instead of letting yourself go and relying on the girdle to hold you up.

One way of taking care of the movement situation is to join a health club. This is fairly expensive, although many of them offer discounts. However, once you have spent the money it might make you use the facilities there regularly. They usually have a nice swimming pool. They also have exercise machines, which I am not too enamoured of, but you can select some which are useful. The trouble with their exercise classes is that nowadays they are madly "aerobic" which means they are better left to the young. Another problem is that the exercise classes are often taught by inexperienced teachers. I have seen ads in the classified section of the *New York Times* which say "young men and women wanted to teach exercise; must be attractive and have good bodies. Experience desirable, but not essential. Will train." The "training" is of the sketchiest kind. I know many dancers who have taken those jobs. At least they have been trained in a dance discipline, and what they teach does have some form. The dancers come and go, since they only take the jobs when they are between engagements. However, one thing you can be sure of is that nothing in their background qualifies them to teach the elderly. If you do join a commercial club select the amenities offered with care. You might enjoy a massage or the sauna. But watch the exercise classes before you decide to join them. Some of these clubs are social rather than therapeutic, and the socializing seldom includes older people.

My hope is that you will learn to enjoy movement and stay with it for good. Movement is the first step to take if you want to destroy the image that has for so many years been the accepted one in this country. Namely, that if you were old you were supposed to stay in dignified immobility. You were supposed to be beyond enjoying anything physical, except eating, I suppose. Anything like sports or sex was thought to be beyond your capacity. Nowadays, I see my older students leading active and often useful lives. They no longer think of age as a stigma. They have learned that age does not cut you off from life. And since movement is life, I hope that many more older people will come to experience the pleasure of movement.

SPORTS

If you have led an active life, played tennis or squash, skied, run, and are generally in fine physical condition there is no reason to give any of it up. However, if you play ballgames, for instance, don't play them to win anymore, just play to enjoy the game. Switch to cross-country skiing and avoid steep hills. Even expert skiers tumble once in a while; the older you get the more dangerous it is to fall. I know an ex-dancer who rides every week at the age of eighty-six; if there are horses in your neighborhood, and you can afford it, get a gentle horse and ride at a sedate trot.

Most sports do offer hazards. If you know how to skate, that's an excellent sport, but there again even good skaters fall sometimes. There are three very good choices open to you. They are golf, walking or hiking, and, best of all, swimming. Swimming is the best thing you can do, but of course, not everybody has access to a pool in the winter or the sea in the summer. This leaves walking, and that too is fine for you. If you really want to do it there is nothing to prevent you. It is up to you as to how vigorous and how frequent you make it.

There is bicycling, a good way to exercise, but here again there is the danger of a bad fall, and traffic does not make it any easier. Besides, older people in most cases see it as something for the young. There are, however, some stationary bicycles these days which are very reasonable in price, and the pedals are adjustable, so that you can "ride" as hard as you like. They look like an X made of two sticks, with a saddle perched at the tip of one, and handlebars on the other, with pedals low down in the middle. I know someone who uses one while watching television.

THE EXERCISES

Since I emphasize stretching so much, if you intend to do my exercises you should get to *like* them. They feel very good and are pleasant to do, and are not difficult. Think of how pleased cats look when they stretch. Try to get the same feeling.

Here is a sample stretch to get you started. You can even do it in bed, and you can point your toes for this one. Lie on your back. Stretch your arms up in a V-shape, keeping them flat on the bed or floor. Keeping your upper body straight roll your hips sideways stretching your arms and legs simultaneously. Reach over and across with one leg. Stretch over as far as you can get. I will take it for granted that you move slowly and do both sides.

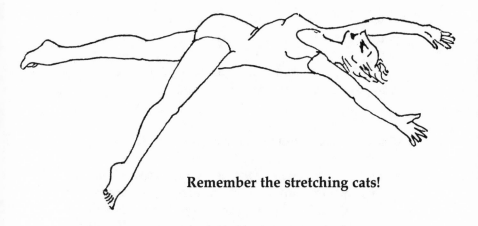

Remember the stretching cats!

Before you do any of the exercises do the following nonexercise. Its purpose is to help you get the *feel* of your body and all of its parts. Lie on your back on the floor or in bed with your arms out, slightly higher than shoulder level. Make sure your hands are *not* palm down. Place your legs about four inches apart. Close your eyes and relax. Then start pressing the back of each hand down on the floor. Next you press each arm down, then the shoulders, then the back of your head. Next comes the most difficult part. Contract your stomach muscles without moving your body. Press the small of your back to the floor. You will probably have to bend your knees to do so. Relax, and do it again. Then try to press your legs down with the knees straight, and finally, press your heels down with the toes retracted.

The reason I am not illustrating all this is because it doesn't look like anything. However, silly as it seems, it will help you control your entire body. The abdominal movement is particularly important since a strong middle is absolutely necessary in order to have good posture, and good posture is essential. If you haven't used your body much for a long time, you most probably no longer feel what the parts of your body are doing. The purpose of this procedure is to get you reacquainted with yourself.

The Right Way to Do the Exercises

Note that the raised arm in the side stretch (A) is fully extended. The palm is turned away from the body and the fingers are stretched as well. The dropped arm is also straight. If you do this movement limply as in (B) and let your arm droop in front you don't get much out of it. The elbow should be *straight* with the arm near your ear.

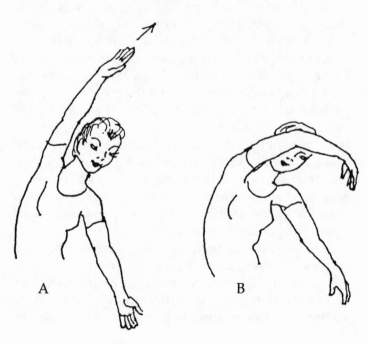

A   B

Whenever you lie on your back with your arms up and out (C) make sure that you try to keep the entire back of the arms on the floor, and be especially sure that the backs of the hands remain on the floor, particularly the part behind the thumb and index finger. This position makes it impossible to roll your shoulders forward, and stretches tight chest muscles. When your chest muscles are tight you can't maintain good posture because they pull the shoulders forward. You may not be able to keep your arms flat at first, but keep trying.

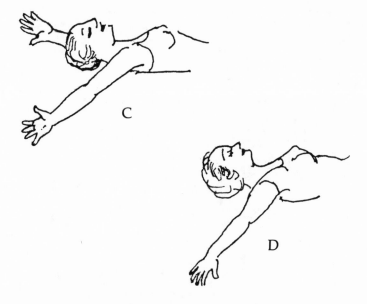

If you put your hands palm down (D) you will find yourself leaning on them and your shoulders will rise off the floor, canceling the chest stretch.

The Effect of Good Posture

Good posture is not only essential for the functioning of your body, but your mirror should tell you what it does for your looks. Bad posture makes even a young body look old. If your posture is bad and has been that way for a long time chances are that you are comfortable that way, and good posture is uncomfortable. Habits are extremely hard to lose. But if you persevere you will lose the bad habit and develop a new good one in its stead. You must become very aware of the difference, and keep at it, no matter how

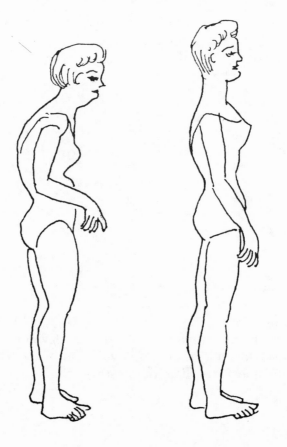

difficult it is at first. It is well worth the effort. Most of the exercises in this book include some form of posture correction as well as the stretching and strengthening that is needed to achieve it. Any body, beautiful or not, looks and functions much much better with good posture.

Attempt at Good Posture (Mistaken)

Most people when asked to stand up straight will do something like the person in this illustration. They

will tilt the head back, overarch the back, and retract the buttocks. This is *not* good posture. It is strained, distorted, and impossible to maintain. It is a favorite of fashion photographers as well as pornographers. For some reason they consider it "sexy." In Times Square there has been a huge sign showing a young woman resting on her shoulder blades and her bottom; she wears two pieces of skimpy white underwear, emphasizing the painfully arched back. This is a typical position, particularly if the model wears little or no clothing. As to why it is considered desirable, I have never been able to understand. It gives me a backache just to look at that sign.

If your posture is not of the best you may have been told by your parents "stand up straight, and put your shoulders back." The result is often like the illustration. Actually, you *do not* put your shoulders back, what you do is lift your sternum, the triangle where your ribs come together, and pull your shoulders *down*, not back. The key to your posture is being able to grow a muscular corset around your middle, learn to hold your head erect, and relax your shoulders, letting them hang down. You will find many exercises here that will help you achieve this permanently.

"Remembering" Good Posture

Good posture means that your head is held up (not tilted back) and not allowed to advance ahead of the body. The shoulders are down and hang free, they are not tight and lifted up toward the ears. There should be a slight in-curve at the waist and the back of the neck, otherwise the back is as flat as possible.

You should feel as if an invisible hand is supporting your diaphragm, lifting the chest, and another invisible hand is lifting your head by the ears, stretching the neck. To help you feel the position turn your hands palm forward and pull them down the sides of your body, staying in contact with your body. You will find that with your hands held this way you *can't* hunch your shoulders, even if you try. If you practice this often you will feel exactly what good posture is like, and in time your body will "remember" it and assume the correct posture automatically.

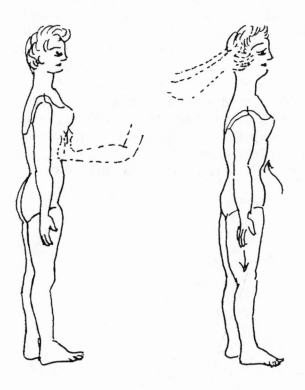

1 Leg Positions, Good and Bad

When you sit on the floor to exercise do not point your feet (A). It looks pretty, especially in a picture, but what you need to do is push the heels forward, and retract the toes (B). You should also straighten the knees as much as you can. You should try to feel the entire length of your legs from the hips to the heels stretching, and the full parts of the thighs and calves touching the floor. If you stretch your heels forward and retract the toes it will help.

You might find that if you sit up straight you have to bend your knees (C). Tight muscles in back of the legs and in your back make sitting at a right angle very hard. Just sitting with your legs straight with your body at right angles to them, your back flat, and your head and chest up, is not easy if you haven't exercised for a long time, and is in itself an exercise even though you are not moving around.

You should *not* look at your knees to see if they are straight, you should feel them. Many people can't feel the difference between a straight knee and a slightly bent knee. Before you do anything else practice stretching your legs, while sitting erect.

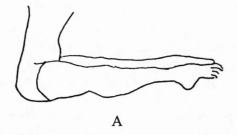

A

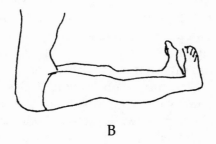

B

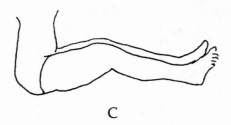

C

2 Learn to Sit Straight

If, when you sit on the floor with your legs extended your position is like (A) it means that your legs are tight from the heels to the hips, and so are your back muscles. You also probably don't have the power in your back and abdomen to overcome the stiffness.

To correct this situation place the palms of your hands on the floor close to your hips. Straighten your arms, and by pushing the hands down on the floor raise your head and your chest and stretch your legs straight while pressing them down on the floor. Raising your head does not mean tilting it back. You raise it straight up and try to lower the shoulders. Practice this until you can do it without the help of your arms. Then do it with your hands on your knees (B).

When you have mastered sitting up straight, start sliding your hands forward on top of your legs so that eventually you reach your feet. Do not duck your head or pull your shoulders forward. You should try to lean forward without rounding the back. Lean from the hips with your head up and your back straight (C). At first you may not get much farther than your knees, but even just trying to get there is good.

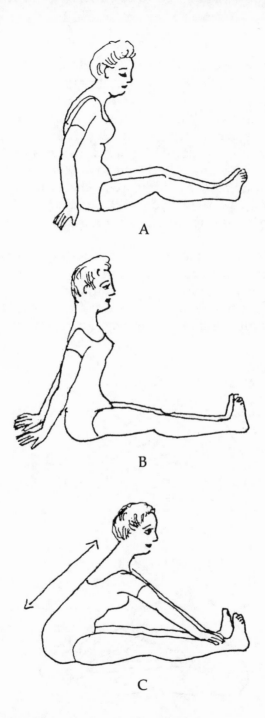

A

B

C

3 Lower Back and Back of Legs Stretch

Sit on the floor with your knees straight, but otherwise relaxed. Rounding your back, drop your head toward your knees and reach as far forward as you can, reaching for your ankles. Next, grip your ankles firmly but do not tighten your arms (A). Lift your head, looking straight ahead of you, then try to flatten your back by lifting your chest and pulling yourself up away from your feet. Simultaneously, flex your feet, pushing the heels further ahead than the toes (B).

This looks simple, but if the backs of your legs are tight, and your back muscles are too, it will prove difficult. If you can't manage to straighten your back in this way, hold your knees and try it. As your back and legs get looser inch your arms down little by little.

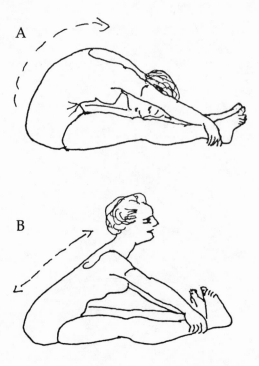

A

B

Basic Chest Stretch, to Be Done Often

This is a basic chest and shoulder stretch. Relax your head, and pull it down with your clasped hands (A). Slowly bring your head back, resisting slightly with your hands. You should feel this in the back of your neck. When your head is well up, pull your elbows wide, as far apart as you can get them (B). Take a slow deep breath. If you work at a desk, or sit for long stretches of time, do this exercise a few times, or even once every hour or so.

A

B

5 **More Complete Chest Stretch for Tight Shoulders**
It is very important to loosen your shoulders. If they are tense and tight you can't possibly improve your posture. Tension in the shoulders and neck also causes pain there and headaches. There is a difference between tension and tightness. Although tension creates tightness, there also exists tightness from disuse of muscles. There are, as well, people who are naturally built compact and tight, and others who, though as flexible as eels by nature, are nevertheless tight

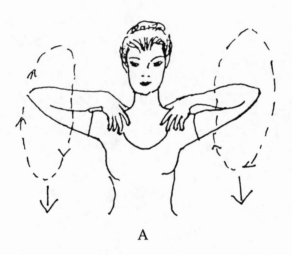

A

because of tension. In any case movement will help the situation.

Place your hands on your shoulders, holding them with your fingertips. Rotate the elbows in as wide a circle as you can manage. On the downward stroke pull your shoulders down. Keep your head erect and your chest high (A). With elbows apart pull one down and one up (B). Now bring your elbows together in front of you, then open them as wide as possible, and lift them up and slightly back (C).

B

C

6 Another Chest Stretch

Grasp each elbow in front of you making a square (A). Take the square and lift it over your head. Don't duck the head. You lift it by pulling each elbow up. Try to keep the square intact (B). Then open the arms wide and bring them down to your sides, palms up (C). Keep stretching your arms as you use them.

You can also strengthen your chest muscles by

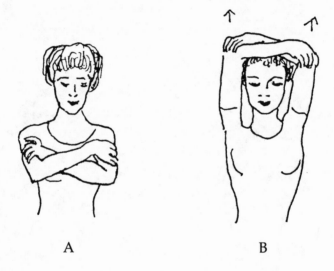

A   B

holding the square up in front of your shoulders and pressing each hand against the inside of the opposite elbow. Press and release several times. This is very useful for strengthening the muscles that support your breasts. You can't exercise the breasts themselves; they don't have any muscles. However, by improving your posture and strengthening the chest, you can help support them.

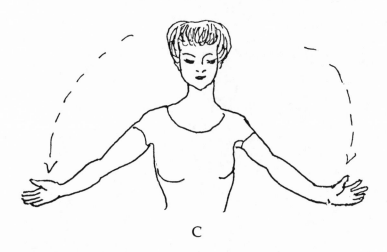

C

7 A Variety of Shoulder and Chest Stretches

You can do these exercises sitting or standing, except (D) for which you have to stand. Keep your head erect and your back as flat as you can. Do not overarch it. With your fingertips touching, bring your elbows up and out as wide as you can. Turn your hands so that the palms face out (A). Next, open your arms wide, turn the palms *up* and bring the arms down to your sides, stretching them as you go (B). Leave your arms hanging freely at your sides with the palms facing forward. Rotate your shoulders, emphasizing the downward movement (C).

Sitting in a straight-backed chair press your back firmly against the chair back. Grasp the back legs of the chair below the seat, and without moving your body in any way, rotate your head, stopping for a second in each position; that is, chest, shoulder, back, other shoulder, chest again. Reverse the circle (D).

Standing as erect as possible bring your arms down behind you and holding one wrist with the other hand pull the arms down, leaving them in contact with your back. Keeping the pull on your arms look over each shoulder, keeping your head straight without tilting it, as if on a swivel (E).

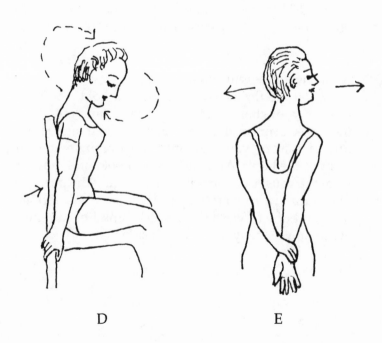

D   E

8 **Using Books for Stretching Chest**
    You can start with paperbacks, and as you improve use some bigger books.

   When you do (B) a variation is to bring the books together in front of you at shoulder level, and then bring them back out. Keep the arms straight.

   With your elbows up and out hold a book in front of your chest. Press your hands on the book as if squeezing it. Hold the pressure for a minute and release (A).

   Take two books of equal size and start with the books touching the floor at your sides. Keep your arms straight and stretched out. Raise the books up until they touch each other over your head. Bring them back down the same way. Do not bend the elbows. Be sure your palms face forward (B).

9 **More Stretches with Book**
    Sit on the floor or on a chair, and hold a book in front of your chest with the elbows up and out. Turn the book over so that the backs of your hands are turned toward you and only the thumbs show in front of the book (A). Holding the book, and moving from the waist up, and without changing the position of the arms, turn your body so that one elbow swings back and one forward (B). I don't think I need reiterate to move slowly and do both sides.

10 Adding Entire Body to Chest Stretch

Another way to stretch to help achieve good posture is to place your palm and part of your forearm on any hip-high object and walk away from it, bending forward and holding your head up by looking at your hand. You walk back until you make a right angle, with your torso parallel to the floor. You then drop one hand trying to reach the floor without changing your body position. Make sure that you are not bending the elbow of the arm that supports you. Try to get a straight line from that hand to your hips. You do that by leaving your palm on whatever you find to support you and walking back with tiny steps until you feel the stretch through your body from the heels to the supporting arm.

11 En Passant Stretch in Doorway

All you need for this exercise is a door. Place your hands at either side of the door jamb keeping them flat and a little higher than your shoulders. Keep the arms straight, and your head straight up. Pretend to step through the door. This is a powerful stretch for the chest. You must never force it, but you can't help feeling it.

Start with your arms at shoulder level, then try to inch your hands up higher a little at a time.

You can do this stretch in another way. Stand in the doorway with your arms in the same position and lean forward with your body held straight and your head erect. Since you almost certainly have a door, you should do this often.

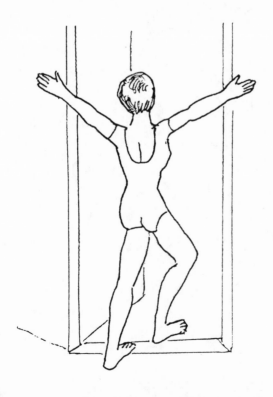

12 Opening Chest by Turning from Side to Side

Stretch your arms out slightly higher than your shoulders, and keep the hands bent up at a sharp angle, palms out. Keeping the hips still swivel the body from the waist up, keeping the head up and still (A).

Return to the center and stop; put your hands behind your head and stretch the elbows apart (B). This exercise doesn't only stretch and expand the chest (don't forget the deep breath when you pause with your hands on your head) but uses the entire upper part of your body.

A   B

13 **Concentrating on Lower Back**

Get on your hands and knees, your hands slightly ahead of you. Drop your head and arch your back like a Halloween Cat (A).

Flatten your back and lift your head. Don't bend your elbows. This movement is meant mainly for your back, and incidentally for the abdomen.

It is very useful if the ubiquitous lower back pain (without any known cause) is your problem. Many backaches, often mysterious, are caused by tension and bad posture (B).

This is an ancient and well-known back exercise and in Yoga it is called "cat and horse."

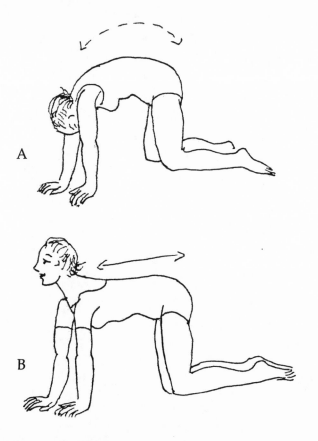

A

B

14 **More Lower Back Movements**

Begin on your hands and knees. Leaving your hands ahead of you sit back on your heels. Keep your elbows straight, and actively stretch your arms forward along the floor as you move back (A).

Keeping your elbows straight, lift your head and chest and bring your hips down toward the floor. Don't try to bring them all the way down unless you are so flexible that it happens spontaneously, which is unlikely (B).

Resume the position on the hands and knees. Turn your hands in so that the fingers face each other. Bend down with your head up, leading with your chest. Try to touch your chin to the floor (C). Return to the hands and knees position.

This is a further development of the "cat and horse" preceding it. You should do both of these even if your back is fine. It's a good form of insurance for keeping it that way.

A

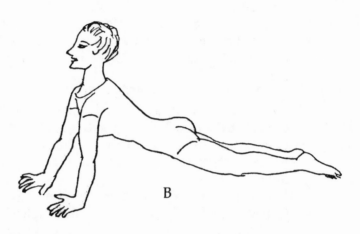

B

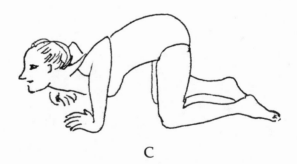

C

15 Stretching in Bed (A)
Stretching Each Leg (B)
Resting Exercise (C)

This is a wonderful stretch to start and end the day with. You lie on your back with your arms extended up over your head. Working on the same side, you slide your arm up while pulling the leg down heel first. You will get a nice stretch through your middle (A).

Lie on your back. Keep your head and the entire back flat on the floor. Hug one leg to you and stretch the other leg straight up. Try to really straighten that leg (B).

This is both a good resting position for a tired tense back, as well as an exercise. You make it into an exercise by contracting your abdominal muscles, and pressing the small of your back firmly on the floor, while stretching your arms up and out along the floor (C).

After you have done (B) enough times to feel comfortable doing it, hug both knees and stretch both legs up. When your legs go up, put your arms straight out on the floor, with the palms up. You should feel the small of your back touching the floor throughout.

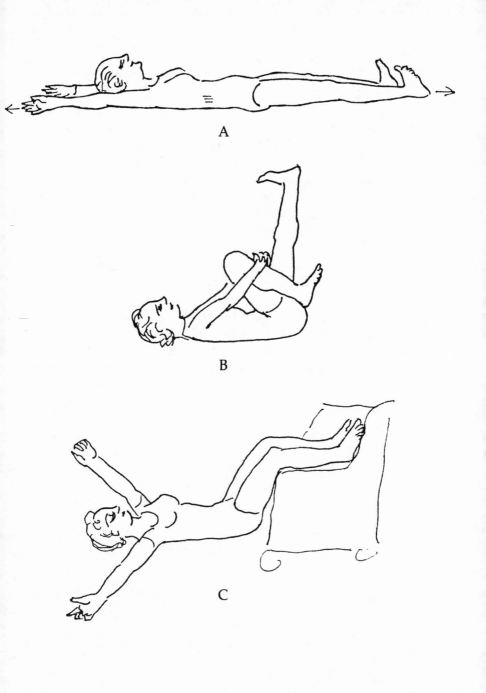

A

B

C

16

Strengthening Back and Abdomen

Lie on your back, arms out, knees bent, feet on the floor close to your bottom. Raise your hips up as far as you can, and bring them back down with your arms outstretched. Try to bring the waist down before your hips touch down (A). Stay there feeling the small of your back in contact with the floor (B). Next raise your head and shoulders and reach for your knees (C). When you do floor exercises you might want to make an exercise mat. You can make one by getting a slab of foam rubber two inches thick, twenty-four inches wide, and four or five feet long. Cover it with a washable fabric, or use a folded blanket. You do not need an expensive mat.

You will notice that many of my exercises involve the back and abdomen as well as other parts of you. This is not an error. The more you strengthen your middle the easier it gets to maintain good posture. The more you use this part of your anatomy, the better.

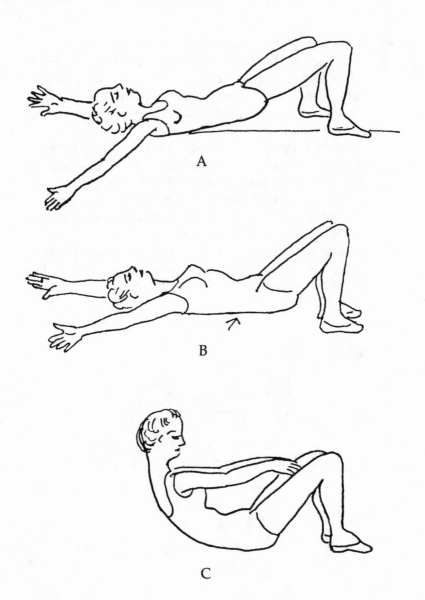

A

B

C

17 Back and Abdominal Exercise with Leg Stretch

Sit on the floor, knees bent, feet on the floor about a foot ahead of your bottom. Hold onto your thighs behind the knees. Don't bend or tighten your arms, leave them loose. Pretend you are trying to lie down, but your arms won't let you (A).

Sit up straight, and stretch your legs straight ahead. With the help of your arms make your back as flat as possible, raise your head and chest (B).

Most people, when they first try this movement, are apt to do (A) by leaning forward instead of hanging back. They also bend the elbows. You should relax your arms and suspend yourself on them. Try not using the arms at all. Learn to use your body with no help from them, that is, for the first part.

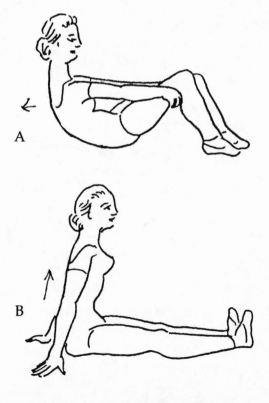

A

B

18 Reverse "Touch the Floor with Straight Knees"

This is the reverse of "bend down and touch the floor without bending your knees." Bend your knees and put the palms of your hands on the floor (A). Straighten your knees as much as possible (don't jerk or hurry). Leave as much of your hands as you can on the floor. They will "peel" off at first, but if you persist, you will find yourself touching the floor with your knees straight (B). This is a basic exercise. Do it as often as possible.

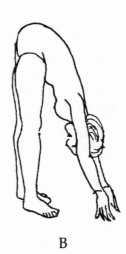

A   B

19 Back Strengthening

Stand with your feet apart. Bend your knees and round your back, drop your head, and leaning your hands on your legs drop down as low as you can (A). Straighten your knees, lean your hands on them so that your arms support you. Lift your head, advance your chin forward, and flatten your back as much as

A   B

you can. Bringing your chin forward as well as your chest will make it easier to get your back straight (B).

Do not do (C) until you have mastered (A) and (B). Keeping your position as in (B) release your arms and let them hang freely. Do this only after you have strengthened and stretched your back by doing the other exercises first.

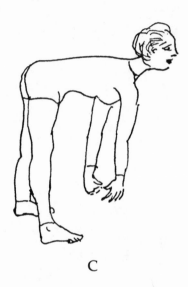

C

20 Back Stretch

Keeping your back as flat as you can slide your hands down the front of your legs, reaching as far down as possible. Do not duck your head, or round the shoulders (A). Lean on your arms on the way down. When you are as far down as you can get relax your body, keeping your knees straight, and let your head and arms hang. Start returning to a standing position, not all of a piece, but one vertebra at a time beginning at the small of your back. The last thing to

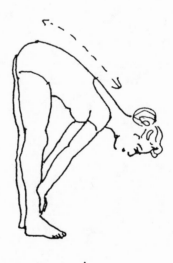

A

come up is your head. You begin this movement by contracting your stomach muscles (B). When you are erect raise your arms straight up, palms forward, and stretch them up. Try to get a straight line from your fingertips to your feet (C).

When you first begin to do this you might have trouble reaching straight up with your arms. If that is the case, concentrate on the chest and shoulder stretches. Tight shoulders are a very common problem.

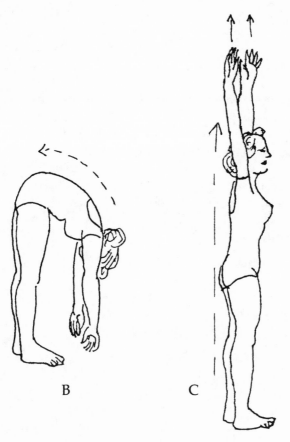

B   C

21 Abdominal Exercise with Book

In order to have good posture you have to learn what your abdominal muscles are doing, and learn to control and strengthen them. Your back and your front work together. If either one is weak or the back is tight it will be hard for you to maintain correct posture.

This silly looking exercise will make you feel your abdominal muscles. Lie on your back, arms out, with your feet on the floor. Put a book, or any reasonably heavy object that won't slide off, on your belly. Contract and release it without involving the rest of your body. The book should rise and come back down.

22 Abdominal Exercise with Book—More Advanced

This set of exercises is primarily for your abdomen, but it is equally effective for legs and feet. Lie on your back, knees bent, feet on the floor, arms relaxed at your sides, palms up as usual. Put a flat book between your knees and straighten the legs without dropping the book, (A) and (B). Now, hold the book with your feet and raise them the same way, (C) and (D).

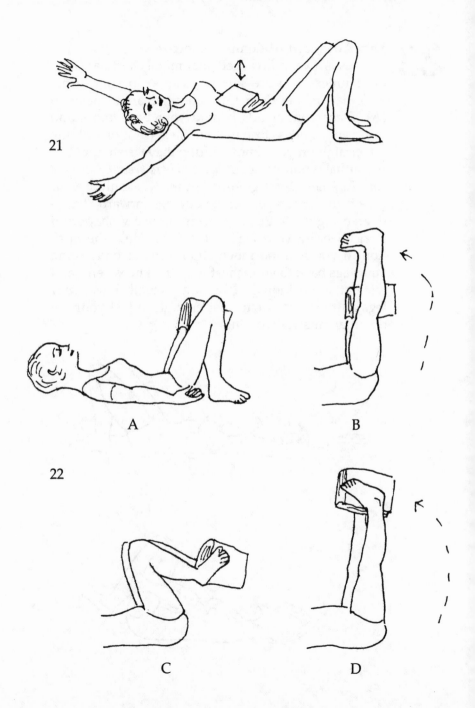

21

22

A

B

C

D

23 **Very Advanced Abdominal Exercise**

This is a very advanced abdominal exercise. Don't do it unless you are *sure* you can keep your entire back flat on the floor throughout. Start in position (A). Place your hands behind your bent knees and bring your knees close to your chest (B). Still holding on, straighten your knees, lifting the legs straight up. If you have doubts about *being able to keep the small of your back flat*, don't go any further (C). Only if your back is under control, bring your legs forward at a 45-degree angle (D). Put your arms out in a V-shape and start lowering your legs to the floor. Hold the position. If you feel too much strain in your body bring your legs back to your chest with the knees bent, and rest in that position (E). You don't actually lower your legs all the way down. Just enough to feel your abdominal muscles working.

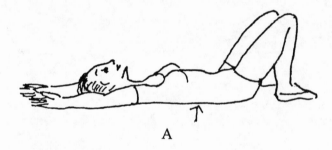

A

B

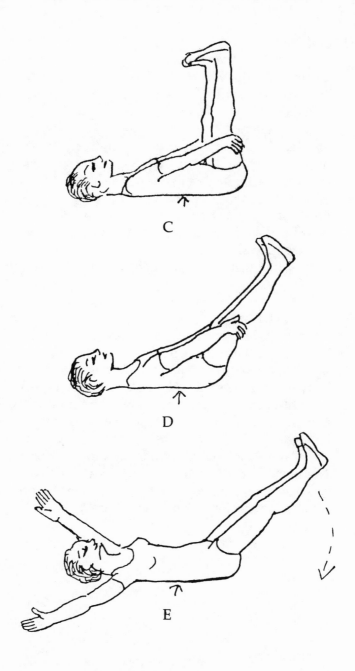

C

D

E

24 **Balletic Stretch**

The sides of your body are not used as much as the rest of you. For that reason, since you want to improve your entire body, you need to do some side stretches.

This balletic exercise is a good way to start. Place one hand on a solid piece of furniture, stretch the other arm up, and stretch the leg on the same side as the raised arm diagonally back, reaching for the floor with a strongly arched foot. Simultaneously, the opposite shoulder swings back and down, and you turn your head as if trying to see your extended foot over the dropped shoulder.

Naturally, as I have said before, you do both sides.

25 **Side Stretch**

Stand with your feet well apart, the toes slightly turned out. Raise the arm and bend the knee on the same side. Keep the other leg straight. Bend your body toward the straight leg. Place your hand on that knee tilting your body over it. Stretch the raised arm and the straight leg. Turn your head to look at the hand on your knee. Keep the entire movement on one plane. Don't let your body lean forward or back. The muscles at the sides of your body don't work as much as the rest of you, so it is a good idea to include some side stretches in your repertoire.

24

25

26 **Balletic Plié**

The first part of this exercise is called a plié in ballet. You hold onto something substantial. Place your feet wide apart and turned out. Bend both knees, keeping your back as flat as possible, making the knees go out to the sides instead of forward (A). Next, straighten your knees and stretch sideways making sure the raised arm is straight, turned away from you, and is reaching over. You will feel that the arm position that I use so much has a good reason.

A

When you turn the raised hand outward you use the underneath part of the arm, from the shoulder to the arm pit. You normally use the biceps much more; the underarm does not do much. That is why so many women when they are older have unattractive loose flesh in that area (B).

When you do the plié, put pressure on the *outside* edges of your feet, to keep your ankles from pronating (rolling forward). This will keep your arches up, and prevent putting strain on them.

B

27 **Stretch with Doorknob**

You stand with the feet about eighteen inches apart and hold the doorknob of a door, either wide open, or locked so that you can pull on it. Keeping your knees straight, swing your hip away from the door so that you feel the pull. Stretch the other arm over (turned out, as usual). You should look like a bow and arrow, your body being the bow, and your arm the arrow. You will probably find that you have a tendency to bend your knees when doing this. Concentrate on keeping them straight. You stand on the outside leg, lifting the heel of the other. You do not move your feet, they stay in place. You pull away from the door knob by moving your hip sideways. Relax the arm you are hanging from, stretch the other one up and over. Turn your head to look over the lowered shoulder.

28 **Diagonal Back and Leg Stretch**

Sit on the floor, put your legs as far apart as you can get them comfortably. Keep your head up. Place your hands on the floor behind your hips. Reach over with opposite arm to touch the ankle, or foot if you can reach it. (If worst comes to worst, touch just below the knee.) After you can do it easily with practice, raise the leg off the floor to meet the hand.

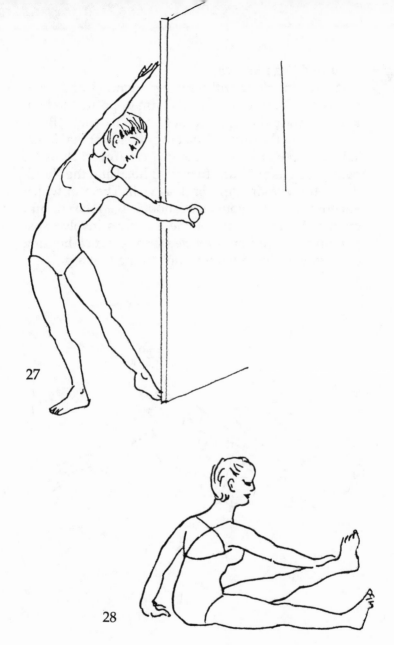

27

28

29 **Modified Yoga Stretch**

Sit on the floor with one leg extended, the other one bent. Reach over with the arm opposite the bent knee, outside the leg, and hold onto its ankle. Brace the elbow of that arm against the outside of that knee. Take the free arm out in a big circle and reach as far behind you as you can. Turn your head and the shoulder of the working arm back as well. The arm which anchors you to your leg should be relaxed and stretched. Since many of the exercises involve suspending yourself on a relaxed arm, practice holding on with your hand without tightening that arm.

30 **All-over Stretch**
    Sit with your legs out as far as you can get them, knees straight. Put your hands on your knees and slide them down toward the feet. Don't round your shoulders or drop your head. Bend forward from the hips (A). Straighten, place your hands on the floor behind you, pull your chin up and lift your chest (B).

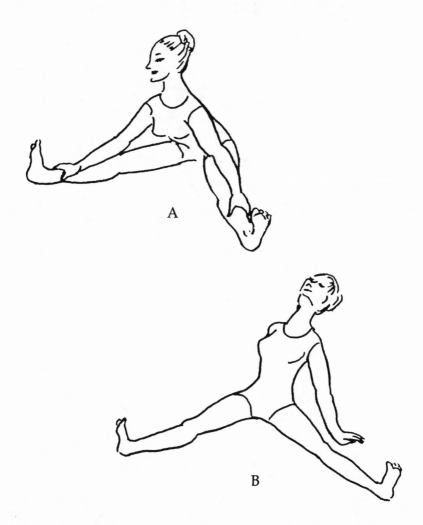

A

B

31 All-over Stretch with More Abdominal Control

Sit with your legs apart, knees bent, and feet on the floor. Hang onto your knees and hang back, pulling your stomach in, dropping your head, and pulling back from your knees strongly (A). Sit up straight, lift your head, expand your chest by stretching your arms out and up with the wrists bent up at an angle (B).

A

Don't forget, whenever your chest is expanded, take a deep breath through your mouth, and let it out slowly through your nose.

This, and the two preceding exercises, are general overall stretches to do as punctuation marks in be-tween more specific ones as you like.

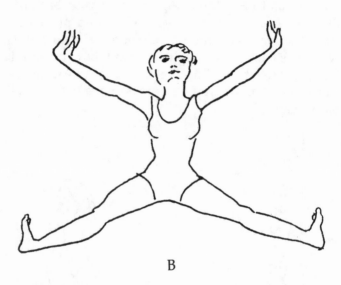

B

32 Using a Wall to Keep Back Flat

A stretch of bare wall is excellent for doing exercises. Lean your back against a wall, your feet enough away from it to allow you to press your entire back against it. Keeping your back and head plastered to the wall, stretch your arms up as close to the wall as possible. Bring your knee up. This will help the small of your back to touch the wall. Stay there a few seconds so as to feel the straightness of your back (A). Bring your arms down to your sides and push away from the wall with the outside edge of your hands. Nobody's back is as straight as a wall, but you should try to feel what you did to get it flat. Your head should stay as erect as when it was pressed against the wall. Step away (B).

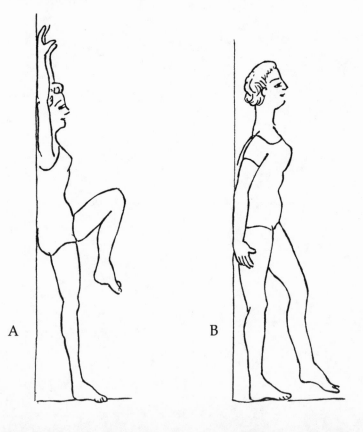

A   B

33 **Using a Wall for Side Stretch**
Brace one arm against a wall at shoulder level with the elbow straight. Pull your hips sideways away from the wall and reach up and over with the other arm. Keep your knees straight. Put your weight on the outside leg and let the inside one trail.

34 **Back of the Arm Strengthener**
When you leave the wall, push yourself away by pushing with your arms straight and held close to your body. Use only the outer edge of your hands. Bend the hands up from the wrists and make the palms face each other. You will know what this exercise is for when you do it.

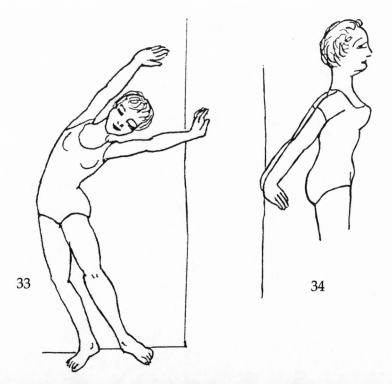

33   34

35 **Lower Back and Thigh Strengthener**
Stand with your back and arms as flat on the wall as you can get them. Your feet should be a foot or so away from the wall. Slide your body down keeping it pressed against the wall until you are sitting on nothing. Push back up, after staying "seated" for a few seconds. Stay down as long as you can. This is a fairly tough exercise. Start at first by just pressing your back flat and sliding down a little. As your back and thighs get stronger, you should get all the way down into a right angle.

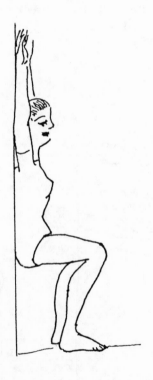

36 **Posture Check**

Stand with your feet about six inches away from a wall. Put your arms up and out, and press everything from the hips up and your arms against the wall. Be sure waist is touching wall. Bring your arms down to your sides keeping them extended and in contact with the wall. Slide the arms back up.

37 Small of Back and Leg Stretch

Stand facing the wall. Place your hands on it at shoulder level, arms straight. Brace yourself with your arms, contract your stomach muscles, and lift your toes off the floor so that you are standing on your heels. Make the contraction of your abdomen stretch the small of your back.

38 All-over Stretch and Strengthener

Stand at arm's length facing a wall. Place your hands on it at shoulder level, fingers turned in. Bend your entire body forward, do *not* lean from the waist. Your body should stay in one piece absolutely straight. Keeping your elbows up and out, touch your chin to the wall. Keep your heels on the floor and bend only at the ankles. Push back away from wall with your arms. This exercise is especially useful after a long walk, as well as before it. If by any chance you are jogging, it is especially important that you do it before and after running. You should also do some leg and back stretches in the bathtub.

39 **Back of Legs Stretch**
Start as in the preceding exercise, but this time come up on your toes as high as you can. Stay on your toes until your chin touches the wall (A). Lower your heels to the floor *before* you straighten back up. (B). If you wear high heels a lot, this one is for you.

Since this is primarily a stretch for your calves you should do it after the preceding exercise. Walking and running use the calf muscles a lot, so they often get sore afterwards. Stretching them helps prevent soreness.

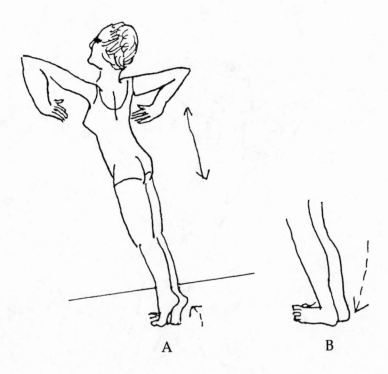

A   B

40 **Thigh Strengthener**

Stand with your feet apart, place your hands on your knees. If you have to lean forward to do it, do so, but try to stay straight as much as you can. Rock from side to side by bending each knee in turn, and straightening the other one. At first do it with your feet slightly turned out. After you are able to do it easily, turn your feet straight forward. It is good for your thighs, especially the inner sides. You can also do it bent over and holding your ankles. That is much harder, so sneak on it by moving from side to side upright first, and once you feel it getting easier slide your hands down your legs until you get to your ankles. This is another good exercise to do in connection with walking or jogging.

41 Good and Bad Chair Posture

Most public seats are enemies of good posture. For some reason they are built so that they tilt you back, and if you spend a lot of time sitting in them, you relax your body and pull your head forward to see what is going on (A).

If you keep the same position of the head when you stand up, you get results that look like (B).

(C) If you habitually sit in that kind of chair, place a cushion or pad behind your back and press your

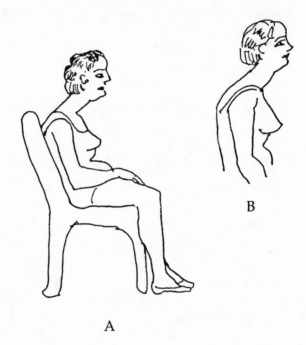

B

A

back against it so that you are sitting up straight. A lot of damage is done to posture when you sit. It is a natural impulse to sort of collapse into yourself and let the chair back hold you up. If the chair back is at the wrong angle, the results are as above. This is often true of car seats, and in public transportation. If you drive often, adjust your seat so that you are sitting straight and don't need to pull your head way forward to see where you are going. If your seat is not adjustable you can get a special drivers' backrest.

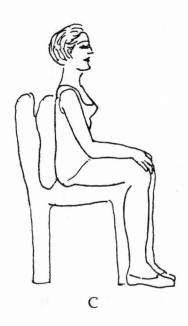

C

42 Strengthening Back, Including Knees

You can do some very effective exercises when sitting in a straight-backed chair. Hold your head up, press your back against the back of the chair, particularly at waist level. Press your feet firmly down on the floor. Be sure that you are sitting way back on the chair, so that *your* entire back is in contact with *its* back. Without moving your body see how far down you can reach by sliding your hands down the back legs of the chair. You will find that you are automatically raising your chest and contracting your abdomen as well as your thighs (A).

Keeping the same position as (A), stretch one leg forward. You can make this exercise stronger by hanging a small weight in a bag on your ankle. As your knees and thighs get stronger put a heavier can or whatever you are using as weight in the bag. This is especially good if you have a knee problem (B).

43 Shoulder and Chest Stretch

In the same position as the preceding exercises, hook your elbows behind the chair back and stretch your hands, fingers apart. This is a powerful stretch for your shoulders and chest. Make sure your head is erect, although actually this movement makes it very hard to pull your head forward and down. If you remember to add a deep breath to it, you will feel your lungs expanding. If you lead a sedentary life do it often. You will be surprised at how much you can exercise without leaving your chair.

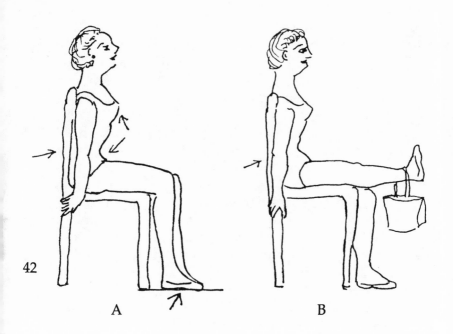

42

A   B

43

44 Leg Stretch on Chair

Put the chair with its back against a wall so that it won't slide out from under you. You can use a heavy chest of drawers, or a couch, that will stay put. Keeping your body erect step on the chair with your hands on your knee (A).

Press gently on your knee, try to get it straight. If you can't do it, find something lower to do it on. If it's too easy, find something higher. After your legs are well stretched keep the knee straight and reach for the top of the chair back (B). I keep harping on leg stretches because they are very important. If your legs and your back are tight, there is no way you can achieve good posture. And good posture is the key to body control.

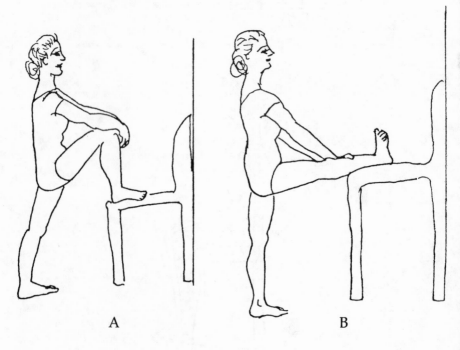

A   B

45 **Abdominal Control**

Lean over the back of the chair, placing your hands on the seat. If it is an average type of chair your abdomen will rest on it (A). Contract your abdomen without lowering your head, and try to lift your middle off the chair back. You will have to arch the small of your back like a cat to do it.

(B) I find that most people, when I first see them, haven't the remotest idea as to what their stomach muscles are doing. That is why I give you a choice of several exercises. Try them all, and you will find out which one you feel the most. Then vary them, but concentrate on the one which is best for you. I find that this one works well for most people, since it gives you something tangible to work with.

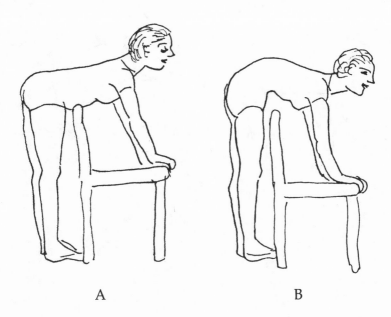

A   B

46 More Abdominal Control

Still in the same position, stretch your arms up and out (A). Bend over and reach for your feet. Don't drop your head. After you are as far down as you can get, contract your stomach muscles, and try to make a space between it and your thighs (B).

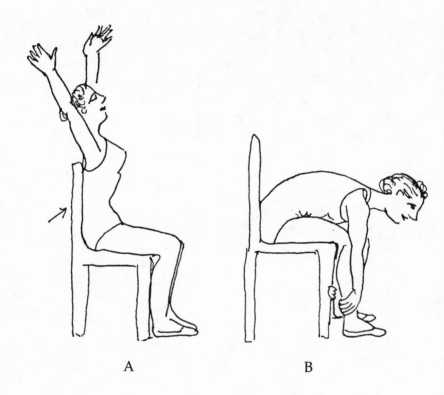

A   B

47 **Back and Leg Strengthener and Stretch (Advanced)**
Without changing your body position on the chair, pull the knee up as close to you as possible (A).

Hold onto the back legs of the chair. Raise one leg straight forward, then bring the other leg up to join · it (B).

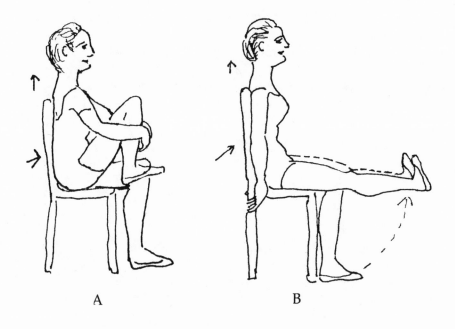

A   B

48 Basic Stretch in Bed

This is a basic exercise that I use in all my classes. Lie on your back with arms extended, palms up as usual. Try to keep your hands and arms flat on the bed or floor. Bring your knees up as close to your chest as you can, and roll them as high as possible on each side. Don't let the feet touch the bed, or the floor, if you prefer doing it there, or if your bed is too narrow to put your arms out. You begin with your arms out at shoulder level; as you improve so that your knees touch the bed at your sides, and your arms stay flat, you start inching the arms up until they make a V.

When you first do this stretch you will probably find that your arms have to come up off the floor, or bed, when your knees move sideways. Don't worry about it, if you persevere they will eventually stay down flat. When they do, it means you have taken a big step forward.

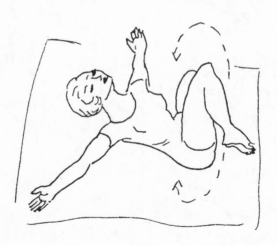

49 More Stretching in Bed

This is another all-over stretch that uses the entire body and feels wonderful. Make your hands into fists, and place the backs of your turned-down fists on the sides of your neck below your ears. Pull your elbows up and out, while stretching your legs and feet in the opposite direction. Make sure the heels are pulling your legs down vigorously, not your toes (A).

You can exercise very nicely without getting out of bed. If your bed has a headboard (most beds have one), you can do this comfortable stretch. Lie on your back. Raise your arms and press your palms against the headboard. At the same time stretch your legs and feet in the opposite direction (B).

All these easy uncomplicated stretches make you feel how pleasant it is to feel your body. If you do nothing else, do them before getting up in the morning, and before going to sleep.

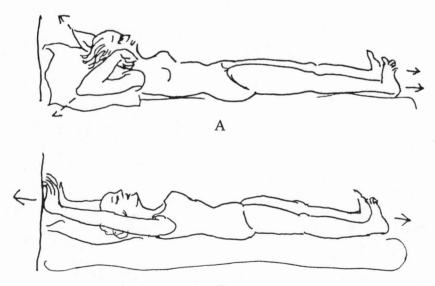

A

B

50 Stretching in Warm Water

When you take a bath you have to stay there for a while so you might take that time to do a few exercises. The ones in the tub are easier to do, since the warm water relaxes the muscles. Sitting in the tub, brace your feet against the front of it, and bending your knees while keeping your back as flat as possible reach for the faucet (A).

Holding onto the faucet try to straighten your knees (B). Lie with your back against the rear of the tub, and lift a leg to stretch it (C). Still leaning back, stretch your legs and turn your feet out, and then in (not illustrated).

There are many stretches you can do in the tub. You can look at the ones you do on the floor, and adapt them to the bathtub. If you are unusually tight, you would do well to start doing such exercises in the warm water first.

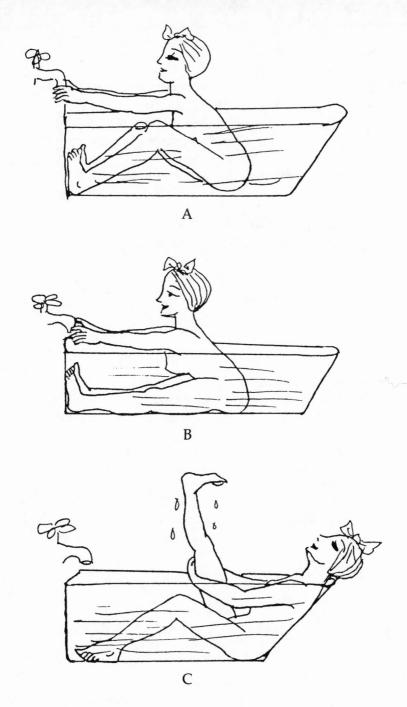

A

B

C

51 **Stretching with Towel**
While drying yourself put the center of the towel behind your knees, bending them slightly, and pull on the towel until it is taut (A). Next, keeping the towel taut, lift your head and straighten your knees and back (B). Since you have to dry yourself you might as well make an exercise routine of it.

52 **Back Strengthener with Towel**
Lift the towel up over your head, stretching it with your arms straight, in a wide V-shape. If you can, keep the stretch while bringing the towel down behind your waist. If you find this difficult, just keep stretching it up until your chest muscles allow you to do so.

53 **Chest and Side Stretch with Towel**
Keeping the towel stretched up, tilt your torso to each side, lifting the heel of the foot of the leg you are leaning over and stretch that leg.

You can also stretch each arm back (keeping the towel stretched) while turning your head to look back over your shoulder. Still keeping the towel taut, bring it down to the floor in front of you. Bend your knees if you need to, then straighten them, and come back up.

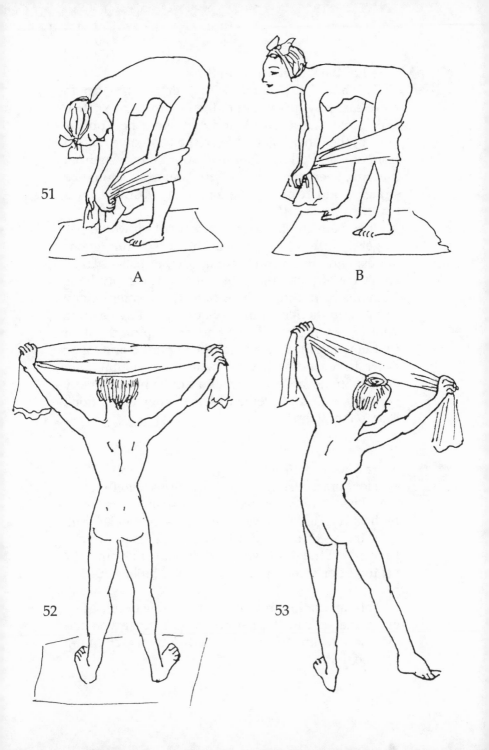

51   A   B

52   53

54 Small of Back Exercise with Sink

This and the three following exercises you can do more easily by holding onto the bathroom or kitchen sink. Hold onto the sink and place your heel on the knee of the other leg, and keep the bent knee high in front of you. Pull the middle of your body away from the sink, keeping your head up. Your arms should be straight, and relaxed. The sink is a substitute for a barre.

If you are going to exercise regularly, it would pay to get a barre. They are available in sporting goods stores, and are called chinning bars, or ballet barres. Don't try any chinning, but do try to simply hang from one by putting it up as high as you can reach on tiptoe, and then let yourself hang from it by bending your knees, thereby lifting your feet up off the floor (not illustrated). These bars can be put up and taken down in seconds. They are better than holding onto various immovable objects, and can be put up at any height you find convenient. But of course you don't *have* to buy them.

55 More Sink Exercises

Hold onto the edge of a sink at arms' length. Hold your knees pressed together and rise on your toes as high as you can. Contract your stomach muscles, pull back trying to do so mostly with the small of your back (A). Straighten your knees and lift your toes off the floor standing on your heels, pulling further back (B).

You can do this and the two following exercises by using the sink in the bathroom. Of course you can use the kitchen sink as well. If you own a chinning bar use that.

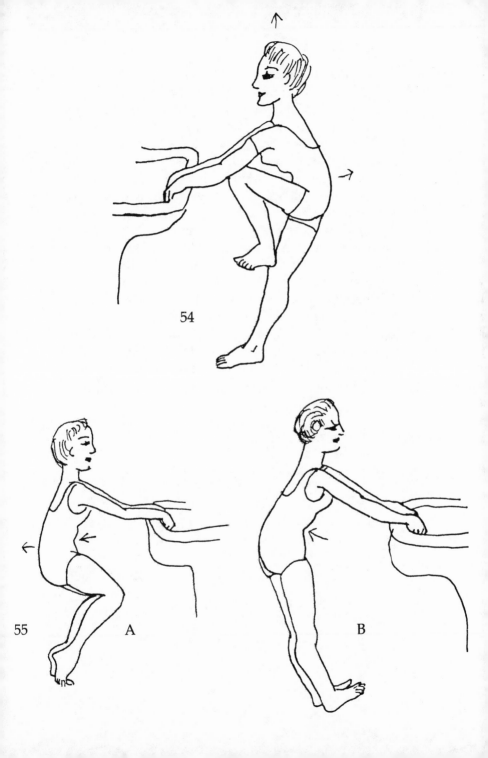

54

55   A   B

56 Back and Leg Alignment with Sink

Hold onto the sink keeping your arms apart, and your head up. Slide one foot back as far as you can, leading with your heel. Bend the other knee in order to allow the other leg to reach as far as possible. You should try to make a straight line from the nape of your neck to the extended heel.

Since you will *feel* what the exercises are doing for you, I leave some of them unexplained so that you will learn what different parts of your body are doing. Until that happens you should just do them to the best of your ability. Just "listen" to your body and you will have control of it. Be patient, it takes time to undo the work of years. Since I know these exercises are pleasant, you should not have any trouble getting to like them. My students often tell me how good they feel after exercising, and how nervous tension and fatigue changes to comfortable relaxation.

57 Back and Abdomen Control

Holding the edge of the sink, bend your knees as hard as possible without lifting your heels off the floor. Round your back and drop your head (A). Lift your head, straighten your knees, and flatten your back. When you are in as much of a right angle as you can accomplish, hang yourself up in that position, without any effort. Your forearms should lean on the side edges of the sink. If you have a barre, just rest your palms on it, don't hold on (B).

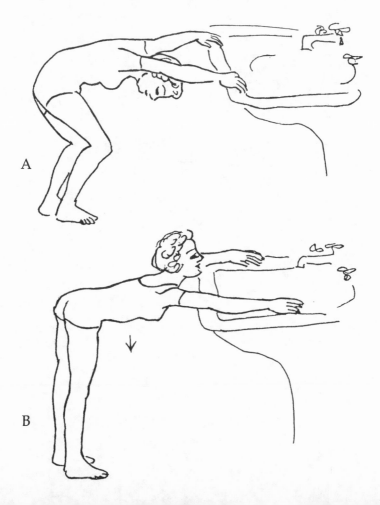

A

B

58 Back of Arm Strengthener and Stretch

This exercise is for the underneath part of your arms (the triceps) which is usually flabby through lack of use. The reason I mention it is that you must *feel* this movement as you do it. If you don't feel it you are not doing it right.

Put the palms of your hands together straight in front of you (A). Keeping your head erect, lift your

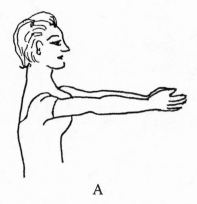

A

joined hands up over your head and slide them down as far as they will go behind you. The elbows should stretch up and the arms stay close to your ears (B).

Bend your hands sharply and lifting your arms back up over your head, straighten your arms, keep them close to your body, and bring them out behind you as if pushing something away from you. Keep the arms close together (C).

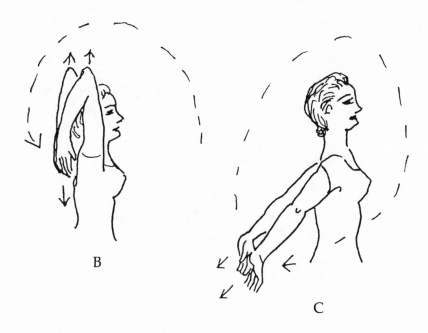

B

C

59 Hand Exercises

You would probably think that your hands get enough use as it is without needing to exercise them. But there again their movements are apt to be limited. What they need most is stretching.

Lean the tip of one finger on the palm of the other hand and stretch each finger back as far as it will go, but never to the point of pain (A). Spread your fingers as far apart as you can put the fingertips of both hands together so they match. Lift your elbows up and press the hands together keeping the fingers straight. Keep the wrists high. You should feel a strong stretch in the palm and the inside of your fingers (B). Place the knuckles of one hand in the palm of the other and press them together (C). Lift each finger up bent as if playing the piano (D). Make a fist and pull the hand downward (E). Make fists and bend the closed hand down then spread the fingers as wide apart as you can (F).

When you are through, let your hands hang limp, and shake them up and down as well as sideways.

It is a good idea to do the hand exercises submerged in warm water.

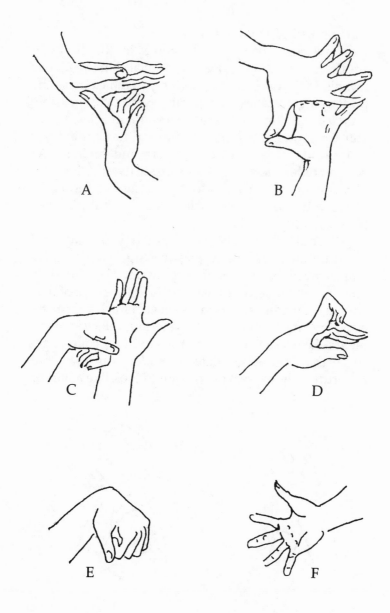

60 Getting Rid of Double Chin

I have seen ads by people who claim that they can eradicate wrinkles by means of "facial exercises." The trouble with this is that although you *can* exercise the underlying muscles of the face, you can't possibly exercise the skin itself, since it has no muscles. When you are young the skin is elastic, and has a thin layer of fat under it so that it is smooth and unlined. As you get older the skin loses its elasticity and the layer of fat shrinks. If you puff out your cheeks and make faces, you *will* use the facial muscles, but *alas*, the lines will only deepen.

The only thing that will tighten your skin and smooth out wrinkles is plastic surgery, nowadays widely available and very expensive. So your only recourse as far as your face goes is to take care of it as well as you can, and don't expect miracles from facials, creams, lotions, or mysterious electric treatments. Learn to live with it. You could, of course, get so fat that you accumulate fat under your skin, but unfortunately the rest of you would look like a blimp.

A

B

The one area where you can make an impression is under your chin. You *can* firm the muscles under your jaw; that is, if you have what is known as a double chin. The silhouette will look better, but if the skin is loose, it will not improve much.

Try these. First and foremost don't thrust your head forward, but instead hold it erect as I have reiterated.

Tilt your head back and open your mouth as wide as possible. Press your tongue against the roof of your mouth, and leaving your head back slowly close your mouth bringing your jaw forward so that the lower teeth are in front of the upper ones (A).

Lean your chin on your cupped hands and try to open your mouth while you resist with your hands (B). Now do the opposite, rest your chin with your mouth open and try to shut it with your hands resisting all the while (C).

Lie on a bed or couch and let your head hang down. Lift your head until your chin touches your chest (D).

C

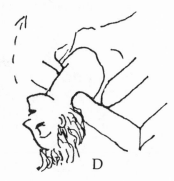

D

61 Foot Exercises

Now we come to the extremities, especially those important and so often abused feet. The feet carry you through life (in the case of women particularly) often crammed into fashionable pointy toed shoes and propped up on high heels, or immobilized by stiff unbending soles.

Your feet are marvelous structures which carry a double load since originally they were used to support the body with the help of the arms when our ancestors walked on all fours. In many cases they are used only one way; that is, for walking, so that they are limited to repeating the same movement, and are hampered even in this by your shoes.

Most people are born with perfectly normal feet, whether high arched or low. The reason for all the hurting feet is that they are never allowed freedom of movement. You can help them, even if they are in bad shape, by making sure you spend some part of every day walking either barefoot, if you have carpets on the floor, or else do it in thong sandals with flexible soles. If you go to the seashore in the summer, walking on sand is very good for you.

The exercises are intended to use all the foot muscles which otherwise are never used. No matter how bad your feet are they will improve if you free them some of the time and do the exercises faithfully. Stand with the forepart of your feet on a book, and your heels on the floor. Hold onto something stable for balance, but don't clutch it, just rest your hands on it. Leaving your feet in this position, keep your body erect and lean forward without lifting your heels off the floor (A). The books should be about two inches thick.

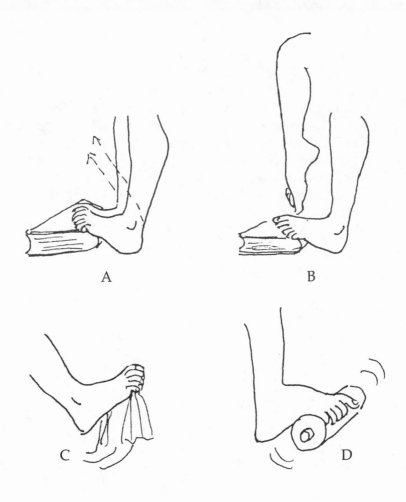

A   B

C   D

Leaving one foot on the book, lift the other one and point its toes as much as you can (B).

Pick up anything you can with your toes, then drop it by spreading your toes as far apart as you can get them (C).

Get a bottle or a can and roll it back and forth under your feet (D).

Turn your toes out and come up on your toes, then lower your heels as slowly as you can. Next do the same thing with your toes straight ahead and the feet parallel, and finally with the toes turned in (pigeon-toed). As you do the last movement roll your feet slightly onto the outer edges on the way up, and straighten them on the way down (E). Lie on your back with the legs straight up (you can hold them behind the knees if you have trouble holding them up) and circle your feet around going one way and then the other (F). You can also do this seated in a chair with your legs straight out in front of you.

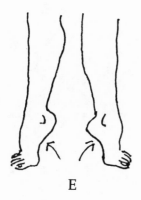

E

F

62

A Stretch That Uses Every Part of You

Simple as it looks you must be able to do it right. The shoulders must not be hunched, the head must be up, and the chest lifted. You should not do it unless you can also keep your legs straight and apart. Leave it to the end.

63 **Rest between Exercises**
An excellent way to rest between exercises, or when your back is tense and tired, is to lie on your back and hug your knees to your chest. Pull them close to your chest, leaving the rest of you flat on the bed or floor. Keep hugging them close and relaxing without unclasping your hands.

Keep moving!